And Then Opens Possibility

Vicki L. Flaherty

www.TurasPublishing.com

And Then Opens Possibility

Copyright © 2017 by Vicki L. Flaherty

No part of this book may be reproduced or transmitted in any form or by any means, graphic, electronic, or mechanical, including photocopying, recording, taping, or by any information storage retrieval system, without the written permission of the publisher.

Photographs © 2017 by Vicki L. Flaherty
Cover: Playa Los Locos, Suances, Cantabria, Spain
Red Barn in Snow: Iowa, United States
Truth's Whisper: Fenore Beach, County Clare, Ireland
Into the Deep: San Agustinillo, Oaxaca, Mexico
Someone to Catch Me: Monte Solaro, Capri, Italy
Speaking to my Heart: Corfu, Greece

Turas Publishing
4833 Saratoga Blvd., No. 129
Corpus Christi, TX 78413

ISBN: 978-0-9832342-6-5

Printed in the United States of America

Dedicated to

all those courageous enough to look inside
to find the possibility that awaits.

Table of Contents

Preface vii
The Red Barn in Snow 1
Truth's Whisper..................... 3
   Truth's Whisper 4
   Today's Opportunity 5
   Beauty in Motion 6
   Unfolding 7
   Flowering to Magnificence 8
   The Simple Everyday 9
   Dancing 10
   Music 11
   Authentic 12
   Open to the Light 13
Into the Deep 15
   Into the Deep................... 16
   Lost 17
   The Struggle 18
   The Vortex 19
   Fear............................ 20
   Where the clouds end 21
   A New Beginning................. 22

Someone to Catch Me **25**
   Someone to Catch Me 26
   Invited 27
   A Prayer for You 28
   Filling Petals with Sunshine 29
   Creating the World 30
   Through You I See 31
   Our Painting 32
   Soft 33
   This Precious Moment 34
Speaking to My Heart **37**
In Gratitude **38**

Preface

When we slow down long enough to hear our inner voice, the essence of who we are speaks, and then opens possibility.

Possibility opens when we are vulnerable enough to be seen and courageous enough to live in integrity.

Possibility opens when we allow both the light and the dark, when we linger in the unfamiliar, and when the desire to be alive drowns out the fear that holds us back.

Possibility opens when we truly see each other and embrace the treasure found in being in relationship.

The Red Barn in Snow

The red barn
standing amid fields of snow
offers hope

Truth's Whisper

Possibility opens when we are vulnerable enough to be seen and courageous enough to live in integrity

Truth's Whisper

My truth
speaks quietly.
It whispers.
Sometimes
it is hard to hear.
In silent moments
of stillness,
I feel its breath
upon me.
Its voice is clear:
Be who you are
completely.
Your light is for giving.

Today's Opportunity

be still
stop striving
just for this moment
allow yourself to soften
open your heart
your mind
your body
invite the gifts of a new day
believe in the possibility that is
YOU

meaning awaits
connection with life beckons
your purpose is alive
and breathing
ready to unfold
today's opportunity
begins with trust
in your grace
your joy
your light
SHINE!

Beauty in Motion

Like a butterfly
Spreading her wings
Engaged in a graceful dance
Floating purposefully
Moving gently forward
Lifted by gentle breezes
Weightless as air
Beauty in motion

Unfolding

the flower bud
unfolds
a slow
gracefulness
joyfully
reaching
and believing

Flowering to Magnificence

The seed,
seeking nourishment,
finds richness surrounding it and
takes inspiration from the light above.

The seedling,
breaking free,
stretches toward the sky and
shouts its greatness to the world.

The stem,
taking shape,
expands into the openness and
develops powerfully each day.

The blossom,
flowering to magnificence,
touches the world with its vibrancy and
shapes the beauty that is life.

The Simple Everyday

I Wake
and I See,
Hear, Feel,
Listen, Speak.

I Look
for Peace,
Wonder, Joy.

I Create
Connection,
Sparks, Pauses.

I Find
Contentment
and Meaning
in The Simple
Everyday.

Dancing

Here we dance.
Our very own dance.

We are small.
We are big.

We are vulnerable.
We are strong.

We are nothing.
We are everything.

We are empty.
We are full.

We are broken.
We are whole.

We are grace.

Music

Your words a song
Your power the beat of a drum
Your grace notes filling the air
A resounding instrument
Your song leads me
To discover
Who I want to be

Authenic

Authentic
Show up
ME!
Real
Just as I am
Nothing to hide
Open and vulnerable
Yet confident and strong
BE
Who I am

Open to the Light

Open to the light
so hungry
to wash over you
and fill the dark spaces.

Listen to the inner voice
feeling its wisdom
penetrate your being.

See the truth
buried under the rubble
of hollow stories
built on the foundation
of fear.

Blossom in gentle acceptance
of who you are
so worthy
of the warmth and love
that waits for you.

Awaken and move
toward the vibrantly alive
life that is yours.

Into the Deep

Possibility opens when we allow both the
light and the dark,
when we linger in the unfamiliar, and
when the desire to be alive drowns out the
fear that holds us back.

Into the Deep

What if
you respond
to the call of the sea
beckoning you
from the safety of the shore
where sand and water meet?

What if
you jump
into the surf
pushing you away
from the familiar solid feel
of your feet firmly fixed
on the earth below you?

What if
you dive
into the heart of the wave
pulsing toward you
shattering you
like a million shells
into grains of sand?

What if
you dare
to move into the endless blue deepness
luring you
into the exhilaration
of the unknown?

Lost

Wandering.
Not seeing the way.
Looking.
Desperately seeking
a path out.
To the other side
of this place.
This thing
that I cannot
figure out.
Despite the light
shining in,
it seems so dark.
Utterly empty.
Alone.
In the middle
of nowhere.
Spinning.
Getting dizzy.
From the corner
of my eyes
scanning for the exit.
Not even sure there is
some place I should be going.

The Struggle

feeling the walls
surrounded in darkness
in the cocoon
no light
only tiny fragments
of hope linger
in the air
like smoke
from a fire smoldering
into the unknown
tension thick
like mud
unsure
what's in here
even more uncertain
what's out there
fear filling the air
wanting desperately out
struggling against the edges
the barriers
holding things in
spinning circles
dizziness pushing 'round
falling to get up
only to sit still
in the gray silence

The Vortex

A powerful force
pulls you in.
Swirling
in an endless tunnel.
No bottom
to stand on.
No end
for rest.
Deep.
Dark.
Only flecks
of light
catch your eye
as you spin
around
and around.
Your arms reach
out
grasping
for certainty.
Your hands
grip
tightly
to something.
Unsure what.
Moving
out of control.

So fast
there's an illusion
of smoothness.
Jagged edges
cut you
as you fall
further in.
You rip
into pieces.
Part of you
lost.
Inside
you hear stories.
They are lies.
You try
to cover your ears.
Despite your repetitive
calming mantra,
the hurricane
continues.
Your fear
hits like punches
against steel.
Hard.
Painful.
Trapped.
You can't break free.

Fear

You speak to me with your tantalizing words.
You tell me I cannot have it all.
You shout at me, vibrating through me:
Who I am is not good enough.
What I want doesn't matter.
You lay yourself in front of me.
You block entry to my soul.
You cover the essence of me in noise.

I miss opportunities when you show up.
You neutralize my relationships.
You suck the reward from my work.

I lose so much because of you.
You steal my sense of wonder.
You squelch my curiosity.
You dismiss my dreams.

May I find the strength
to push you out of my life,
your false sense of importance
and the expectations you create
less real to me.

Where the Clouds End

It starts like the rustling of paper.
As the wind breezes through the leaves,
dust swirls into a gauzy haze.
The skies darken with foreboding.
Gray blackness looms like a blanket.
Ripe round droplets tap, tap, tap.
And crescendo into a deluge.

The storm exhausts herself.
And the rains back away.
Their cleansing work complete.
Silence follows the clamor.

At the line where the clouds end,
the filmy ceiling dissolves into the heavens.
Nourishing waters soak deep into the earth.
Calming light returns anew.
Trees stand steady and tall.
Grasses dance with grace.
Flowers rise to the joyful sun.
Peace lies softly in the air.

A New Beginning

You stand at a point of departure –
a place from which to powerfully transform.

Choice offers itself to you.
Stay here?
Or, courageously step
in the direction of dreams?

What will be lost?
What will be gained?

From a still place within
intentions move to the surface.

Reflection invites clarity –
insight shapes inspired action.

You step into a new beginning.

Someone to Catch Me

Possibility opens when we truly see each other and embrace the treasure found in being in relationship.

Someone to Catch Me

Someone to catch me.
A friend to keep me
from falling.
Offering his hand
that we might take this journey
strong and protected
side by side.

Invited

He listens.
Understands.
Opens his heart
so you have some place
soft to stand.
He wraps himself gently around you
holding all the pieces of you
together.
He asks, what if:
You quit fighting?
You loosen your grip?
You open your palms wide?
You invite the noise and chaos in?
You simply let go?
You allow your heart to speak?
You trust the wisdom of your inner voice?
You own your truth with confidence?
He invites you:
Be who you are,
right where you are.

A Prayer for You

I whisper into the wind
that blows gently off the sea.
I speak of peace
into the frosty white haze.
My prayer released for you
into the blue-gray sky.
My hopes carried by the waves
as they roll back from the shore.

May you find strength like the rocks
that anchor along the beach.
May you feel grace like the birds
who float through the sky.
May you find treasure in today
like colorful shells gathered from the sand.

Filling Petals with Sunshine

Each person you touch
in whatever way
is blessed.
You grace others' lives
in ways that may be
unseeable.

Like God's little secret,
the meaning in our lives
is sometimes hidden
below the surface –
or maybe high above
and out of reach,
for now.

Each time you ask for help,
Each time you let someone give,
Each time you open yourself ,
You exercise your power
to create meaning.

Each time you lean into
your vulnerability,
your purpose unfolds,
like a rosebud
hungry to fill its petals
with sunshine.

Creating the World

Our meeting creates light,
nourishes our souls.
Reaching deep into our roots,
we find our personal truths.

Our conversations flow like water,
sharing the essence of who we are.
Encouraging each other in our growth,
one is sustenance for the other.

Our curiosity anchors us.
Trusting the direction of our hearts,
exploring infinite possibilities,
we relish in the mystery.

Our energy is power.
Bringing our brilliance to life,
shaping our ideas,
we celebrate our discoveries.

Kindred spirits on a journey,
we share a belief
that we can create the world
as we want it to be.

Through You I See

I speak the truth that I see for you.
Only to discover that in really seeing you,
I discover what is true for me.

Our Painting

The canvas white with possibility.
Old expectations pushed off the edges.
Past chapters of life lost outside the frame.
Emptiness waiting impatiently to be filled.
The blank fabric inviting the dreamer.

Stories we want to believe
begin as lines gracing the page.
Emotions we dare to express
create a rich and courageous texture.
Acceptance gently hiding beyond our grasp
dances like shadows on the page.
The power and grace we hold
paints a perfect balance of color.

Like hope rising
boldly from our hearts,
shapes take form
and the picture emerges:
A reflection of our perfect souls.

Soft

you can peek
into her heart.
you might even see
the light
like a halo
emanating around her.
there's kindness
in her actions
and hope
in her words.
her softness
is the heart
of all good things.

This Precious Moment

I look into your eyes;
a deep well invites me in.

I listen to your words;
their syllables envelop me.

I touch your presence;
a palpable energy showers me in light.

Illuminated, you leave me curious.

What awakens your spirit?
What makes your heart sing?
What do you love more than anything?

Here. Now. Together
We live in this breathing, precious moment.

Speaking to My Heart

The circle
with its open center
and soft edges
speaks to my heart
in whispers
of completeness

In Gratitude

I have been encouraged to write since I was a young girl, and it served me well in accomplishing many achievements in my life. What I am only now realizing is what an amazing self-discovery tool writing is. Words and stringing them together helped me find purpose and passion and power. This book came to me slowly. Seeing clearly can take time. It started as inspiring words captured on a page, evolved to phrases, and eventually, took shape as ideas filled with insight and meaning.

I am deeply grateful to all those who inspired and guided me in opening to possibility. These include my husband, Jim Hogan, who is a constant source of love and encouragement; my parents, Gerry and Terry Flaherty, who gave me a foundation of love on which to fully live my life; and Diana Bing, for her light and invitation, and Therese Kienast and the Radical Leadership Team, for waking me up.

I am indebted to the family and friends who reviewed early drafts. They saw my heart and helped me express it clearly: Jedn Bordon, Lisa Flaherty, Liz Hogan, Peggy Kennedy, Jana Mitzoda, Maureen Monte, and Otema Yirenkyi. I also appreciate all those who inspired my spirit - I'm certain I don't even fully realize all the people whose example has touched and shaped me in some way; I'll name a few, however: Minoo Alasti, Adrienne Barr, Katiuscia Barretta, Lori Benz, Lisa DeShano, Mike Flaherty, Dorota Florczyk, Kate Kemp, Teresa Lopez, Lati Modarressi, Diane Painter, Ginny Paulson, Lisa Roberts, Elise VanderMeer, and Blair Wagner. Thank you to my colleagues and community who welcomed my light.

May you listen to your heart as it whispers your dreams.
May you know you are enough, just as you are.

May you find wisdom in even the most unexpected places.
May you move with a sense of grace as you dance
with the unfamiliar.

May you live each day fully, creating heart-full memories.
May you step toward the future that is uniquely yours.

And Then Opens Possibility

by Vicki L. Flaherty

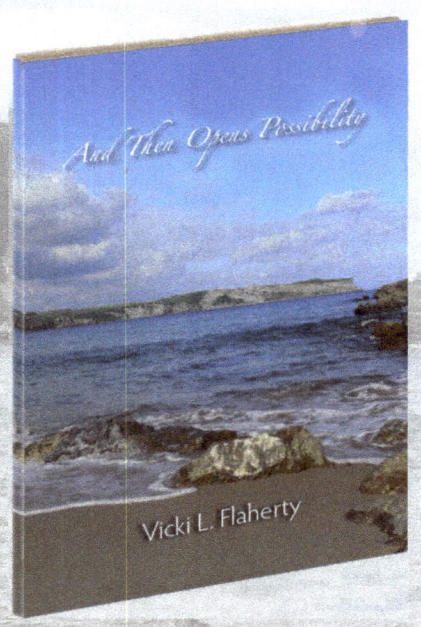

ISBN: 978-0-9832342-6-5

Softcover $18.00+shipping

Order copies of this book by visiting
www.TurasPublishing.com

Also Available from your local bookstore,
Amazon.com, and through Ingram.

Mostly My Heart Sings
by Vicki L. Flaherty

ISBN: 978-0-9832342-0-3

Softcover $14.00+shipping

Order copies by visiting
www.TurasPublishing.com

Also Available from your local bookstore,
Amazon.com, and through Ingram.

www.ingramcontent.com/pod-product-compliance
Lightning Source LLC
Chambersburg PA
CBHW040209020526
44112CB00039B/2851